DON'T LEAVE
LIFE
ON THE TABLE

DON'T LEAVE LIFE ON THE TABLE

Preparing Entrepreneurs for the
Next Season of Life

ANDREW WILLIAMS

Copyright © 2024 by Andrew Williams

All rights reserved. No part of this publication may be reproduced, distributed or transmitted in any form or by any means, including photocopying, recording, or other electronic or mechanical methods, without the prior written permission of the publisher, except in the case of brief quotations embodied in critical reviews and certain other noncommercial uses permitted by copyright law. For permission requests, write to the publisher, addressed "Attention: Permissions Coordinator," at the email address below.

Andrew Williams
andrew@exitwithandrew.com
www.exitwithandrew.com

Don't Leave Life on the Table, Andrew Williams —1st ed.
Paperback ISBN: 978-1-963911-19-0
Hardcover ISBN: 978-1-963911-20-6
Printed in Canada

CONTENTS

Prologue .... *vii*
Introduction .... *xiii*

1. The Challenge 1
2. Untangling the Work Wires 7
3. Accepting Help 11
4. Taking Care of Your People, Part 1 17
5. Taking Care of Your People, Part 2 27
6. The Sojourner Process™, Introduced 33
7. The TALENT Tool 39
8. The TRIBE Tool 49
9. The TIME Tool 55
10. The TREASURE Tool 61
11. Stepping into the Next Season 67

Conclusion 71
Epilogue: If You're Ready To Sell 75
Acknowledgements 77
Resources 79

Appendices

Appendix A: SHAREHOLDERS TOOL 81
Appendix B: STAKEHOLDERS TOOL 82
Appendix C: TALENT TOOL 83
Appendix D: TRIBE TOOL 84
Appendix E: TIME TOOL 85
Appendix F: TREASURE TOOL 86

PROLOGUE

When I left Chris's office on that Friday afternoon, he was walking on air.

We had just successfully negotiated and executed a letter of intent from a Chicago-based private equity firm that was going to not only pay him a very respectable multiple for his company, but the full appraised value for the real estate. In addition, we negotiated that the firm would pay his health insurance until he reached Medicare eligibility age. They even agreed to let him store his boat in the warehouse during the winter. Things could not have gone any better for Chris at this stage in the process of selling his company.

When our conversation was complete, he walked me to the front door of his business. This business was founded by Chris' father, and over the years had become a place that defined so much of his life. Once outside, Chris looked at me - all smiles - and shook my hand saying, "*Thank you so much for everything you've done throughout this process!*" As I walked away from Chris that Friday at 4pm, I felt proud of the work we had done together. He seemed genuinely gratified at the result of the negotiations.

The following Monday morning, Chris called me and terminated our agreement.

Over the course of my experience as a Merger and Acquisitions Advisor, I have learned to arrange all of my client engagements on a month-to-month basis so that my clients know they can trust me for the quality of my work. These engagements, like the one Chris and I had, are also cancelable at any time to avoid clients feeling forced or trapped into any decision. So, at that moment, Chris was well within his rights to terminate our agreement.

However, I was still deeply confused. Given the last exchange we had, where Chris vocalized his delight over the negotiation, I was caught completely off guard. Why was Chris backing out of the transaction? Was he suddenly dissatisfied with the terms, or was there something deeper going on?

Because Chris was the only client that had ever terminated an engagement with me, the question at that moment was "Why?"

After some stunned silence, I said "*Chris, I don't understand why you want to throw this all away. You seemed very happy Friday afternoon when I left and now, you're firing me? What could I have done differently?*"

After a long pause, Chris sighed and said, "*Well, I had never mentioned to my wife that I was thinking about selling the company.*"

"And how did it go when you told her this weekend?" I asked.

"It didn't go the way I thought. I took her out for dinner Friday to tell her the good news and she was very upset with me. She said, 'I don't know what you think you are going to be doing with your time, but I don't want you at home with me, so you'll have to find something else to do to stay busy.'"

Chris continued, "*The more I thought about it over the weekend, I figured I'd just keep coming to the shop. I didn't realize my wife wasn't ready for me to stop working. I'm tired, I'm getting older, and I don't know what my life would be like without the shop. But the problem is, I don't know what else I would do with myself and my time...*"

Despite my experience working with business owners and entrepreneurs of all kinds, at that point, this was a conversation I had never had. Chris was fully ready to exit his business, had found an incredible offer, and then found he wasn't mentally or emotionally ready to pull the trigger.

So, when I fully understood what Chris was telling me, I told him I would cancel the agreement.

I hung up the phone with great sadness over the fact that Chris would be losing out on a fun and full new season of his life because he didn't have the right conversions at the right time. He had prepared the business for his exit, but he hadn't prepared *himself*.

Each day after the conversation, I couldn't get rid of this nagging thought: what if, as an M&A Advisor, my clients prepared mentally, emotionally, and relationally to sell their business just as seriously as they prepared for the financial side of the transaction?

On the day Chris terminated our agreement, he was 67 years old. He told me he had nothing else in his life to do with his time except work, go to the gym and use the boat when the weather permitted. What Chris had unfortunately learned after the transaction negotiations is that his wife didn't want him "at home with her". As a result, he settled for the "same old, same old" instead of embarking on a new adventure. He had plenty of money. He had a general manager that handled 98% of the issues that came up at the Company. But what Chris *didn't have* was a purpose outside of the four walls of his business.

That happened to me 12 years ago, and I've never forgotten that conversation. In fact, to every client that has hired me since then, one of the first questions I ask is, "Does your spouse know you are thinking about selling?" Most of them say "Oh yes! They are the ones pushing me or encouraging me to do so."

I follow that question with "...So what are you planning to do in the next Season of life?..." However, when I ask that question, it is common to see a look of uncertainty in the client's eyes - despite their sincere desire to exit. When that happens, I engage them in discussions not just about balance sheets and leadership teams, but also in a deeper conversation about what I believe is the ultimate question of exiting their company: "What comes next in your life?" If a client is not ready to answer this question thoughtfully and completely, I've learned it is highly unlikely that they will be satisfied with their life or the transaction, no matter how good the dollars, terms, and agreements are.

I decided to write this book because the frequency of these conversations I'm having is increasing. More and more, I find that entrepreneurs appear or say they are ready to move on from their company, however, they have no idea what it looks like to prepare to do so with respect to their personal purpose. This guidebook comes from my hope that you and other entrepreneurs like you don't get to the spot where Chris found himself that fateful weekend.

In his famous book "Man's Search for Meaning," legendary Holocaust survivor and psychologist Viktor Frankl outlined his philosophy that a human's deepest desire is to find meaning in life. If people find meaning, they can survive anything. In his book, Frankl suggests that there are three ways to find meaning in life: *through work, through love, and through suffering*.

While I have no insight into how love and suffering have impacted your life, if you're reading this book, it is likely because your work has given you significant purpose. However, just because you will no longer own or lead your business after exiting your company, it is critical that you *know your days of experiencing purpose in life are just beginning*.

This book is about helping you see the next season of your life as a new *beginning* that will allow you to embrace a new and perhaps deeper purpose. This book will help guide business leaders like yourself through a process that needs to come before the transaction - a process I call the *Sojourner Process* ™.

The Sojourner Process™ is a series of four practical tools that will challenge you to stop worrying about the bottom line of your business, and turn to the mental, emotional, and relational preparation that will result in a life full of purpose when you exit that business. This is work that involves your head and your heart, your family and your employees - and your time, talent, treasure, and tribe. Exploring these areas thoughtfully is the core of a journey - a Sojourner's journey - that I believe is necessary for all business owners to embark on.

So, whether you are ready to engage in exiting your company today or are ten years away from initiating that, welcome to the Sojourner Process™. I hope that the process and tools this book will walk you through are helpful not only to you and your people, but ultimately incredibly impactful on the world itself.

INTRODUCTION

You are bigger and much more important to the world than the company you currently run or are considering exiting.

How much thought have you given this truth?

This is a statement that many business owners lose sight of at some point in the process of starting, buying, scaling, operating, and selling a business. You are wired to have a huge impact on our world and on the places where you find community both inside and outside your business. This is true for all of us on this earth, but especially true for those gifted with leadership abilities, as most business owners are.

While your time and energy may have been heavily invested in the business over the last handful of decades, at some point this will change. *You will not be a business owner forever.* When that is no longer a title you have, who will you be?

In my work with clients, I have the pleasure and responsibility of advising entrepreneurs and leadership teams who are looking to sell their companies. What is interesting to me is that sometimes those decisions happen without significant consideration for what life could and should look like in the "next season."

The next season is the life that lies ahead of you when "business owner", "CEO," "President," "Partner," "CFO," "CMO" (etc.) is no longer a title you have. Many business leadership teams and entrepreneurs are hard-driving, highly intelligent, high-achieving people. If you are wired that way, here is some news for you: after you move on from the role of leading a company, you will not be able to "flip a switch" and simply stop thinking as a business owner. You will *always* be hard-driving, highly intelligent, and high-achieving. This is a good thing - but it's also why it's critical to be <u>moving into</u> something, taking your skills and abilities into the world rather than letting them become dormant or unutilized.

A lack of intentionality around exiting from your business and into something else will greatly impact your perspective on and sense of purpose regarding the life left for you to live on the other side of the transaction.

Because this is a phenomenon that business owners experience in a unique way, I believe it is critical that you *prepare* for it in a unique way.

Data shows there is a significant difference in the satisfaction tied to an exit between entrepreneurs who had been intentional about crafting their vision for that 'next season' and those who were not. The first group usually find excitement, joy, and freedom amidst the uncertainty and change the business sale brings. The latter tend to linger in fear of what comes next, drifting in uncertainty rather than walking away with a sense of greater purpose and often asking themselves "Why did I do this?"

But when you don't have the responsibility of a company's success on your shoulders, that doesn't mean you aren't responsible for making an impact on the world in other ways. All humans are created for a purpose, and yours doesn't end when you're off the payroll.

Take, for example, a conversation I once had with a client named Pat:

"I want the maximum net proceeds as an outcome of this sale," a CEO named Pat told me. "I want to sell all of the operating real estate and empty lots as well".

"Ok, that's good," I said. "But what makes you say it that way?" I questioned.

"Well, my Church is actively building shelter structures and wells in developing countries and all the money I make on the sale is going to fund that mission, in which I will serve".

Pat is just one example of an entrepreneur with a very clear plan for what he was going to do in the next season of his life. This plan involved not only his money, but his time and a community he felt like he was a part of. Pat took the sale of his business and turned it into an amazing opportunity to impact the world.

Whether you are five days, five months, or five years away from selling your business, the good news is that this book outlines a process you can embrace that will help you define this next season of your life. Alternatively, you can also do nothing in preparation for life after you sell your company. With these two options in front of you, think about the following question:

When you are ready to exit your business, what do you want your life to look like?

Of all the ways one might answer that question, my experience has shown me that the majority of business owners would tell you they hope their life after the sale of their company offers them more time, more freedom, and more peace of mind. If you are working with one or more advisors to achieve a well-planned exit strategy, these objectives are likely well thought out and generally achievable – you will likely have the money and the time you seek.

But what about having *more purpose*? This outcome is not automatic. Money can't buy you purpose, and time can't either. Purpose is simply not a natural by-product of exiting your business. *The outcome of finding purpose is a result of thoughtful introspection and planting seeds in your mind, heart, and relationships well before the business exit is complete.*

As you read this book you will walk through a unique process that taps into your perspective as an entrepreneur to help you identify your purpose and put it into action. This process will help you plant and nurture those seeds needed to grow the next season of your life.

<u>**There are hundreds of books about how to get the company ready to sell. This is the only one uniquely developed with a process designed to get You ready to exit from the company.**</u>

Chapter 1

The Challenge

There is an exciting challenge looming out there on your horizon - one I hope you are anticipating with excitement.

However, before you arrive at what that horizon holds, you must embrace the following challenge: as a business owner (or Partner in a services firm), I am going to challenge you to embrace your entrepreneurial wiring as the primary means to finding purpose.

For many business owners, understanding what makes you "tick" as an entrepreneur frequently gets lost in the day-in, day-out logistics of running a company. However, it is critically important to success - both in and outside of your business - to understand what your inner workings are. Among many other things, entrepreneurs are highly driven achievers…but I suspect you may already know this about yourself, right? The question now is what to do with the internal drive you possess. There is now science behind what you have always surmised about yourself. It's outlined in the book "Driven: Understanding and Harnessing the Genetic Gifts Shared by Entrepreneurs, Navy SEALs, Pro Athletes, and Maybe You" by Douglas Brackmann.

Failing to acknowledge the challenges that come with no longer operating your life as a "business owner" ignores a critical part of who you are. This often leads to a place of unhappiness after exiting a business. The way your brain works is unique, and this is not a bad thing. It is part of what has made you so successful in your career, and it is who you are until the end of your days. You look at things and *see what can be*, and as a result, you need to think about how to make the best and greatest impact with your skillset in this next season.

In her book Quit - The Power of Knowing When To Walk Away, author Annie Duke writes: "*When your identity is what you do, then what you do becomes hard to abandon, because it means quitting who you are.*"

Though you have run a successful business, who *you* are and what *your impact on the planet* is reaches far beyond the business that you own today. But how will you ensure your drive for impact comes along with you when you sell the company? By creating a vision for the next season built on the embrace of your entrepreneurial wiring.

All human beings need a purpose. As an entrepreneur, why not embrace and leverage the drive you possess elsewhere? Some entrepreneurs sell a company and then go on to build others. Other entrepreneurs choose to throw themselves into the next season of life in a different manner, pursuing non-business interests. We will talk about both in this book. The important thing isn't *what* you do, it's that you do it in a way that creates a sense of purpose.

The first transaction I closed as an M&A advisor was on behalf of a client that randomly picked up the phone the day I cold-called him. He explained he knew it was time to sell his company because two weeks prior, he had suffered a heart attack at his desk. He was a very entrepreneurial, Hoosier farmer who had started a side hustle, which had unexpectedly grown into a successful $3M EBITDA per year company. In addition, he also never stopped farming. When I met him, his heart (and his wife) had told him something had to give.

He explained to me that the day he woke up in the hospital after his heart attack, his wife told him it "was time to sell the company..." because she "...didn't want it to kill you (him)..."

In that moment, being a business owner was what he knew, but - it was not his only option. In the time that I worked on his behalf, we effectively dealt with this reality. Later, when we met for lunch on the first anniversary of the closing, he told me he was having so much fun living that he "...didn't know how he had ever found time for work!..."

The first step in preparing yourself to exit your company is to embrace who you are as a Human, an entrepreneur, and business leader - *in order to embrace who you'll be when "Owner" is no longer your title on the business card...*

One of the things that makes it difficult for business owners to embrace this challenge is because, in my experience, they don't know how to fully understand and view their business. When I first meet them, my clients who are looking to exit their companies fall into two distinct camps: a) Some see the business as an asset and are actively trying to grow the enterprise value and then b) there is another group, often referred to as owners of a "lifestyle business" where growing the enterprise value isn't necessarily the key objective.

It is important to know which camp you fall into because your tenure at the company and the manner in which you leave will be impacted by the way you see your business in relation to the rest of your life.

I once exited a partnership because I realized my partner was more interested in how the business drove his "lifestyle" than in how we were actively growing the enterprise value. Regardless of which of these two categories you fall into, what is true is that sometimes the business reaches a point where it ultimately defines the owner's life.

Which of these camps do you fall into? If you can't define how your business defines your life and why, you'll struggle to be able to see how you can use your entrepreneurial brain for the coming season outside of your business.

As I said earlier, the impact that you <u>can have</u> on our world is <u>much bigger</u> and better than the business you currently own. It is bigger than the enterprise value your business has at the end of your tenure, and it is bigger than any lifestyle you might adopt. No matter what kind of business owner you are, you can't escape this truth.

The skillset, vision, drive, and determination that are inherently wired in you will be highly valuable in the next season of your life as well, increasing your impact on the world outside of your business from passive to active. Just as you had a philosophy behind your business leadership style and goals for the company in relation to the rest of your life, you must develop a philosophy and goals for what happens next. It's time to begin to imagine the impact on others and the personal fulfillment you will experience in this season of change.

Chapter 2

Untangling the Work Wires

> "Five hundred, twenty-five thousand, six hundred minutes
> Five hundred, twenty-five thousand moments so dear
> Five hundred, twenty-five thousand, six hundred minutes
> How do you measure, measure a year?"
> From 'Seasons of Love' by Jonathan D. Larson

Human beings are wired to work. In this chapter, we will discuss the importance of realizing that work is not your life, and why this is a more urgent realization than you might think.

While the pandemic forever changed the way the world sees work, we can still look at entrepreneurs in every sector and realize that their DNA is a bit different than others. As I discussed in the prior chapter, it's okay to embrace the purpose work gives you, because humans are created to work. But for many of us who own a company, it is hard to "turn off" the work switch - whether you're at the end of a business day or the end of your ownership part of a career.

If you worked 40 hours a week, 2000 hours a year, from age 20 to 65, you would have worked 90,000 hours. I'm guessing that readers of this book would typically work more than that – say 50 hours+ - which would equate to greater than 108,000 lifetime hours of work. That is a lot of time dedicated to your chosen profession!

In the previous chapter, I highlighted the truth that entrepreneurs see their business in different ways. However, after spending hundreds of thousands of hours during a lifetime building a company, a business often becomes more like a home for many people. The business and their office are a comfortable, safe place, and going there each day is *beyond what they do, it's who they are.*

Not only because many entrepreneurs are so driven, but more so because many of them mainly identify themselves as "Founder/Owner/President of XYZ Corporation," my clients often have a difficult time "untangling the work wires" which keep their mind and identity chained to the job. But once you've tackled the challenge of embracing the way your brain works as a business owner, it's time to untangle the wires so that your ability to find purpose isn't attached to your business, but to *whatever* you put your talent and skills towards.

It is truer today than ever before that business owners are retiring later in life. This is in part because they haven't prepared themselves to let go of the business.

Going back to the 2008-09 great recession, it was expected in the Merger and Acquisition markets for privately held companies that there would be a 'catch up' period in 2010-12, when the owners that had planned to sell in 2008-09 finally would. Interestingly, that wave of activity never materialized.

However, because Father Time and Gravity are still undefeated, eventually a large percentage of America's privately held companies will transition ownership in the next decade.

Business owners who will sell in this coming wave of transitions, like you, have the ability to be better prepared. It is time to begin untangling the wires that drive you to work, so that you're ready to find purpose beyond your company. It's wonderful that your work has brought you purpose, and it's time to expand that into your next season of life.

Why is it so important? For starters, it's literally a matter of life and death.

In October 2016 The Harvard Business Review published an article titled "You're likely to live longer if you retire after 65.[1]" Then, in July 2018, Forbes published an article titled, "How early retirement might be killing men.[2]" That article states:

"There is also suggestive evidence that males engage in more unhealthy behaviors once they retire," the researchers wrote. "In combination, the results suggest decreased labor force participation upon turning 62 as a key reason for a discontinuous increase in male mortality, although other factors may also play a role."

---

[1] https://hbr.org/2016/10/youre-likely-to-live-longer-if-you-retire-after-65
[2] https://www.forbes.com/sites/johnwasik/2018/07/09/how-early-retirement-might-be-killing-men

Both articles ultimately get to the same root issue – *a life best lived requires a purpose – ALL Human beings need a purpose*.

My objective in the Sojourner Process™ is for you to realize it can extend beyond the role you are exiting. As Viktor Frankl's work teaches, for entrepreneurs like yourself, knowing your purpose in the next season of your life – before exiting your company – may literally be a matter of life and death.

For yourself and for those who you love, it is time to start thinking about these things. However, it can be daunting to begin this process. In the next chapter, we will discuss one major reason business owners end up working themselves almost to death: it's hard to ask for help when it comes to transitioning out of your business.

Chapter 3

Accepting Help

> "I get by with a little help from my friends...."
>
> – The Beatles

In 2011, the Exit Planning Institute published a study showing that 75% of entrepreneurs regretted their decision to sell their company. Every other year since, when the Study is completed, I'm shocked at how high this number is. I do, however, believe there was incomplete preparation that resulted in a less than perfect outcome for many of those that were polled.

The EPI study cited three main responses:

1. They felt it didn't accomplish their objectives,
2. They didn't understand their options.
3. They had no plan for what to do after the exit.

Can you think of a time in your life where you ever set out to be in the lower 75% of any group? I highly doubt it... Truth is, most entrepreneurs aren't successful by settling for "status quo." However, if you aren't willing to accept help from others, be it a business coach, exit planner, or M&A Advisor, you may likely end up as one of the 75% of business owners who are unhappy with their exit.

Why? Because of a failure to ask for help and seek counsel in preparing for one of the largest, most complicated, emotional transitions of your lifetime. *Thinking about the sale of your business with the next season of your life in mind will keep you out of that 75% of unhappy former owners.*

As discussed, we know that our nation's business owners and entrepreneurs are driven and highly motivated – so how is it possible that 75% of them missed the mark on this critical life decision? It seems crazy that three out of four highly driven and intelligent entrepreneurs are swinging and missing when it comes to the sale of their business – how can this be?

My friend T. Ray Phillips has been an exit planner since 1998 in the Indianapolis area, and he has an excellent perspective on why business owners are unhappy with the sale of their company. T. Ray believes that there are two key reasons why business owners don't ask for the help needed to prepare for the sale:

1. Many business owners aren't aware that services to help plan for their exit/sale exist. If they do know there is help available, they don't know where to go and ask.
2. Many entrepreneurial Leaders struggle to ask for help and instead feel the burden to figure it all out on their own, no matter how impossible that may feel.

T. Ray is a wise man and once again here is exactly right. It's not a lack of time and resources that causes business owners to inadequately prepare themselves for the sale, it's that they don't know help is available, and that they often think asking for help is a weakness.

What is the root issue keeping a business owner from getting over either of these hurdles? It boils down to the truth that **human beings don't like to talk about endings.** Addressing the barriers listed above requires facing the reality that your involvement in the business will eventually end, and you need help navigating that. If this is a reality that a business owner has absorbed, they will likely be more willing to actively seek help, and even be excited about finding it.

In Tom Dean's book "Willing Wisdom" he provides the astoundingly low number of Americans that have an estate plan or 'will and testament'. Why might that be a reality? It's because as human beings, we love to talk about new, better, and shiny stuff, but we don't like to talk about *endings*. I'm guessing you haven't pre-planned your funeral, have you? We typically don't even begin a vacation by thinking about the day we'll go home, do we?

We often shy away from the reality of what is ahead of us, for fear that it will ruin the moment. Too many business owners are applying this logic to the exit of their company. If they don't ask for help to sell the company, or for help to prepare for the sale, they don't have to think about the business-owner season of their life ending. You will not be ready for the sale of your business or the next season of your life if you aren't courageous enough to talk about closing the chapter of your business.

Renee Russo is both an EOS Implementer and CEPA certified Exit Planner. On this subject, Renee notes:

> "The term 'exit' seems to have been misunderstood. When you 'exit' a cinema, you leave the cinema to go somewhere else, you open the door to what is next... the exit is not the 'end', it is the beginning of what is next...The entrepreneurial journey is at times an emotional roller coaster ride. Although the idea of exit planning may be initially met with resistance and fear of the unknown, the real risk is in not doing it at all... When managed well, the exit planning process will align the goals of the Owner at a personal, financial, and business level.
>
> The exit of a company is a complex and deeply human journey, and it is important that real consideration be given to the time, thought, and care needed to move through the process effectively. Business owners are preparing to "hand their baby over" to someone else, they are preparing to not see the faces of some of their closest friends at work every day, and they are preparing for the fact that they need to remember who they are at their core and design a life that they desire on the other side of that 'exit' doorway.
>
> The more empowered that a business owner is to see the ending of their time at their company as the beginning of a new journey, the fewer regrets they have when it is all said and done. It is far scarier

> *to continue to run your business without a plan for your future in place. If you want to stay in the driver's seat of your life, work with a business coach and advisor to ensure that you have a road map to deliver what you really want in business and in life."*

So, if you are afraid to talk about the ending of your time at your company, it's time to ask yourself this: What if what's on the other side of the exit is just as wonderful and purpose-giving, *if not more so?*

When you exit your business, there is so much more life *ahead* of you. There is nothing to be afraid of. Are you open to accepting the help you need to embrace the next season of your life? Thinking about the "ending" of this current life chapter is a **requirement** to starting a fresh, new beginning.

It's time to shift your mindset - it's time to make a 180° change in your view of this next season of your life. Because what comes in the next chapters of this book isn't about an ending – it's really about an amazing new beginning for you. The point of the Sojourner Process™ is to have a method, a process, and a conversation about how to get to that amazing new place. But you can't do it unless you are willing to acknowledge the need for help. Your best outcome will be found if you don't walk through this alone.

The next chapter will discuss taking care of your "two teams": family and work. Once you know how these two groups truly matter to you in this process, you will have a clearer understanding of how to move forward, because you'll understand the whole picture. You'll understand that your purpose is about more than you, and your impact extends into the lives of others. This will never be more true than it is during this key transition point in your life.

Chapter 4

Taking Care of Your People

Part I: Family

You've heard it so many times, it's become a cliché: "Make sure your mask is on and oxygen is flowing before helping others." The point is that as a leader you are best able to help others when you are firing on all cylinders yourself.

At this point in your journey through this book, I'm assuming that you've challenged yourself to accept your wiring as an entrepreneur. You've begun to untangle your drive to work at your company into a drive to have purpose elsewhere. And you've begun to build up the courage to think about the ending of your time at your company. But what about the impact of all this on your family and employees? This is the last step you must take to prepare to engage in the Sojourner Process™ productively, *where you truly flesh out the vision for your next season*. It is critical to undertake this piece of groundwork to think about how you can best lead your people, both inside and outside of the company, when you exit.

As a leader to both your personal and your work families, it is your duty to think about "your people" as part of your exit process. By doing so, you will thoughtfully and intentionally set them up for success in your exit process which will benefit your sense of purpose on the other side of active involvement in the Business. Though you will spend time thinking specifically about the different communities *you* want to invest in as part of the Sojourner Process™, the purpose of this chapter is to get you thinking about how and why your family and employees will be affected by the entire transaction process.

As a leader, you have a responsibility to ensure they are affected positively. Doing this intentionally will leave you with a strong sense of gratification and purpose as you step into the next season knowing you've given appropriate consideration to the impact on those around you.

Okay, but what if you fail to do this? What if you choose to skip this chapter – not just the book, but also of your life – and blow forward to the next thing...

Shareholders vs. Stakeholders

In a presentation I frequently give to groups of business owners, I ask the question "*What is the job of a publicly traded CEO?*" Pretty quickly, someone usually answers "To grow shareholder value."

After seeing nods around the room, I then ask, "*What is the job of a CEO of a privately owned business?*" After what is typically a much longer pause and a couple of other answers, someone will inevitably say *"It's the same job...the same thing,"* which is true.

The good news is that owners of private companies typically have a greater ability to consider their stakeholders, not just their shareholders.

Not only are owners' views of the purpose of their business often incomplete, but their views of who the business impacts are *also* typically incomplete.

As you already know, your business doesn't just have shareholders, it has stakeholders. The ones that may come to mind easily include your family, your employees, your community, your customers, and your vendor base. You need to understand and clarify who those stakeholders are, and how the selling of your company will impact them.

If you've done some work to define what the core values of your Company are and are actively using those core values to hire, fire, recognize, and reward your team, then you may be further down the road on establishing the bigger purpose for the business, who the stakeholders are, and what is a transaction that is consistent with those core values and addressing your true stakeholders.

Your Company and entrepreneurial journey are about more than money, right? It's about people...and you often only get one shot to show them you care about their stake in the game during this transition.

Here's the first tool to help you think through this: spend some time identifying who you think of as different categories of stakeholders, why that is, and why your next season of life will impact them. Once you've done some brainstorming on this, we will discuss some of the nuances of the most common groups of stakeholders: your employees and your family.

share·hold·er
/ˈSHer‚(h)ōldər/

noun
noun: **shareholder**; plural noun: **shareholders**; noun: **share-holder**; plural noun: **share-holders** an owner of shares in a company.

stake·hold·er
/ˈstāk‚(h)ōldər/

noun
plural noun: **stakeholders**

a person with an interest or concern in something, especially a business.

denoting a type of organization or system in which all the members or participants are seen as having an interest in its success.

Instructions: Take some time to clear your head and use the tables in Appendix A and Appendix B to identify who you consider both your Shareholders and your Stakeholders. The following table is an example of how the tables can be used.

SHAREHOLDERS and STAKEHOLDERS

Name	What do they Deserve	Name	What do they Deserve
Kristin	More of my Bandwidth & heart	Leadership Team	these past weeks have humbled me with their passion
Kids	Me undistracted – learn to be fully present with them	Full Team	What could make a real impact?
Advisory Board	sure, I've paid them but what do they TRULY deserve?	Joe	I need to make things right with him
		Dad	How much time do I have left? No time to waste here
			** Need to spend more time on how to impact the full team's life

Stakeholder First Team: Your family

Now that you've thought about who your stakeholders are, it's time to recognize and address that there is a cost to being an entrepreneur that sometimes doesn't show up in a financial statement. Unfortunately, that cost typically is the impact on relationships closest to you, most frequently your family.

Regardless of how your family relationships work, they'll be impacted by your exit process, and they will matter when it's finished. You must have conversations with your family members about preparing to exit your company that address the following questions:

- Will your exit from your company impact your family dynamics and how you spend your time together?
- Will your exit from your company change their role in the family business, if they are involved?
- Will your exit from your company financially impact your family members (i.e. children and spouse)?

Understanding our relationships with both our family members and stakeholders, however they look today, is critical to achieving a sense of peace in this process by knowing you have considered all those that you care about who are impacted by your decisions in this journey. If you address the topics above before you exit, the process will go much smoother and your relationships with your family members will be functioning and healthy on the other side of the sale of your company. These relationships may currently exist both in and out of the company itself, and I urge you to think about both.

Do you have your next generation or even two generations of family working in the business? If so, one of the most important things you can do as you think about exiting your company (now or down the road) is make them go work somewhere else for a period of time.

Here's the rationale: in your market, or in other places nearby, there are incredibly well-run businesses with practices and culture that your business would do well to emulate. Why not have your kids go work there, learn from great companies, and leverage those practices back at the family business? Doing this will also encourage your family members in the business to build a sense of personal identity that is larger than the family company, which will positively impact them, the family, *and* the company. By working elsewhere, family members will also develop a strong sense of empathy for other employees, which is critical to being a strong leader.

As you well know, your business impacts your family members who are involved in both positive and negative ways. As a leader, you are charged with setting *them* up for a maximum sense of purpose when you leave. This includes employing them to be strong, strategic, and empathic leaders.

A second thing you need to think about before you begin your transaction, as it relates to preparing your family relationships, is how and when you will engage them in conversations that address the questions listed above. In a later chapter, we'll talk a little bit more about exit planning and advisors, who play a crucial role in helping you to invest the time to get these key parts of a transition well-documented and thought through. Family in the business and family outside the business need to know what is going on, and you need to have a dialogue with them about how it will play out.

I've met families who were preparing to engage me to sell the company who no longer have Thanksgiving dinner together because of business-related feuds. That is a sad thing to see and should also be avoidable if the entire family feels included and informed on these business decisions. However, it does require some hard or honest conversions to be had.

A client once failed, despite my urging, to share with their adult children what the financial impact of the sale of the family business would have on their lives. None of the children worked for the company, but they assumed they would receive some of the proceeds upon the sale. You can imagine their shock when they discovered the vast majority of the proceeds would be going to charity because the client felt they already had plenty of money. Unfortunately, the children's shock turned into strained relationships with my client. Though they would have been disappointed to some degree in any order of events, the impact on their family's relationships would have been miniscule had they known far in advance that the business proceeds would go to charity. It is precisely these kinds of conversations that business owners need to proactively anticipate - I cannot stress this enough.

Apart from managing expectations, it will take a weight off your shoulders knowing your family feels as though they are a part of the process, and your relationships will be intact at the end of it all. Though it may be uncomfortable, familial conversations about your exit plan are a part of setting your family up for success and empowering them to benefit in whatever your purpose is after the sale.

The Sojourner Process™ will change you as a result of you gaining a vision for what is next, and as a result may create change for your family as well. I often remind clients (and my family) that life *is* change and there's nothing wrong with that. However, failing to have these conversations can result in major but unnecessary implications going forward. Please don't ignore the need to have the right conversations with your family.

CHAPTER 5

Taking Care of Your People

Part II: Employees

Now, let's discuss the importance of spending time preparing your work team for your exit from the company. There are two basic questions you need to ask yourself to do this:

1. How do you thank them for what they have done for the Company while you were the owner?
2. Who is the best 'next owner' and what opportunities does that create for your people?

In the early stages of being engaged by a client, they typically begin by saying, "I don't want the people at the office to know this is happening." All advisors working on sale transactions and exit plans highly respect the need for confidentiality when we work with our clients. However, there is a difference between subjects that are confidential, and subjects that are just uncomfortable. Telling your employees you are beginning the process of exiting the company falls into the latter category. So, when a business owner tells me they don't want any employees to know about their exit, my general response is, "You don't hire dumb people, do you? Whether or not you'd like to admit it, your employees are thinking about when you will exit the company. They are also likely talking about this - and wondering what you are planning to do - with their peers and families, and wondering how it impacts them."

You cannot appropriately thank your employees for their work under your leadership or fully prepare them to succeed in *their* next season - when you are gone - if you do not let them know that you are engaging in conversations about an exit plan. If you choose not to do this, you may say "thank you and good luck," as you leave, but I promise your employees will certainly not feel thanked, prepared, or particularly lucky.

These may feel like challenging conversations to have, but the reality is that your silence on the topic makes the process worse. You don't need to share every detail of your transaction process with them, but if you share pertinent details relating to how the sale will affect them, you will gain a sense of confidence and fulfillment that you are leaving your work team as best prepared as you can to succeed after you leave.

Now obviously, the makeup of your leadership team, family vs non-family, will also impact the way you go about this, but be conscious that your team is talking about this to each other, whether or not you are talking to them about it. It's okay to tell them you "don't plan to die at your desk" and that you are working with people to execute a plan.

Your employees are counting on you to do this well. Your team typically has a wide range of tenures, some folks have been with you a long time while in the post-COVID years you probably also have a decent amount of relatively new faces. All of them are counting on you doing this well so their work life is disrupted as little as possible. They also want you to do this well because they respect you as a leader.

One of the things for you to consider in this process is what part of, if any, of the proceeds do you plan to share with your team. There is no rule of thumb for this because every business is unique in the makeup and tenure of the leadership team.

As an example, one great tool is the "stay bonus." This is a set amount of money you would share with each key member of your leadership team. They are awarded half of the money on transaction day, and the second half of the money after some predetermined period under the assumption that they haven't quit. This type of arrangement creates a leadership team that is fully incentivized to make sure the business continues to grow and performs on a trend equal to what the buyer is expecting. This often helps to assure that you receive a full payout on any seller note or earnout arrangements. (Of course, if the leadership team member is terminated by the new owner without cause, they should still be eligible to earn their stay bonus.)

If you think about these things thoroughly and have the conversations early in the game, your employees will feel your gratitude for their tenure, and they will be incentivized to help the company grow when you leave.

The second part of taking the best care of your work team involves who is the next owner and how do they align with your current employees. If you are transferring the business to your Family or the current leadership team, this is relatively easy. If you are going to transfer externally, this highlights one of the value propositions that an M&A advisor brings. They will fully vet the market of potential acquirers, not just with respect to the financial element, but equally if not more importantly - with respect to who is the best cultural fit. The next owner should be the person who also provides the best opportunities for your team when you're gone.

I once sold a client to the U.S. arm of a major Corporation that was based in the UK. There were five partners with the older partner owning majority control and the four younger shareholders who were staying each held minority shares. This large strategic buyer was the highest financial bidder in our process, yet the four younger partners were hesitant to sell to the largest player in their industry. That was until they fully understood what the new salary structure, benefits, and opportunities for career growth were going to be. Then they realized it really was a win-win for everybody and we executed a great transaction.

The important thing to remember is that life is going to change for everyone involved – sometimes a little, sometimes a lot. Don't ever use the phrase "nothing is going to change." Even if the acquirer only changes the color of the sign, that's change! As you know by now, some people struggle to deal with change in life. After the business is no longer under your control, you won't have an impact on how much change does or doesn't happen. So, take advantage of the influence you have now to thank your employees well, financially or otherwise, and provide them with the opportunity to grow and develop under the next leader.

As we now move into the Sojourner Process™, take a moment to reflect on these two important groups: your family and your work team. Yes, the point of the process you will soon walk through is to discover YOUR purpose in the next season of your life. However, these two groups are likely a huge part of the purpose of your business, and your leadership has impacted them greatly. Please trust in this statement, and return to it as motivation:

> *The sense of purpose you draw from both the current season of your life AND the next season of your life will deepen when you know you have sufficiently prepared your family and employees to grow and succeed in the wake of your exit from your company.*

Having thought through these truths and understanding that your purpose in the next season of life is much bigger than you and your company, it's time to begin learning and utilizing the Sojourner tools.

Chapter 6

The Sojourner Process™, Introduced

Whether this book was given to you by someone who cares about your future, or you picked it up on your own, the fact that you are holding it suggests you are at the starting point of a fantastic new journey - a journey toward *the next season of your life*.

Once you have first begun thinking about exiting your current company, you are officially a "Sojourner." A Sojourner is defined as someone who is "staying as a temporary resident." Though you are beginning this journey into a place of unknown and personal reflection now, the objective is to not *stay* where you are – this is a temporary stop on your way to living out the vision you will take some time to create. It is important to not get bogged down by the details, and to begin acting on the ideas you have already and are about to develop. This is what will help you move forward.

As we have discussed in relation to the sale of your business, life is about change. Today, whether you feel great, poor, or somewhere in between about where you are, the only certain thing is that your life won't stay the same as it moves forward. The great news is that you already have the ability to envision and intentionally move toward what is next – the objective here is simply to draw that out of you.

The Sojourner Process™ is a specially designed method to intentionally cast a vision for how you will use your unique skills and gifts in the next coming season. As a Sojourner, you will work through four tools to understand and create how best to leverage the unique drive that entrepreneurs and leaders have in the season of life after you exit this business. You may have heard some of the concepts before, but the Sojourner Process™ is about viewing basic areas of life from the perspective and experience of a business owner.

The hope is that you will use these tools to help you embrace being a temporary resident in all the stages of life. The steps in the Sojourner Process™ are designed to help you open your mind to a new vision and thoughts that you're often not able to consider when you're deep in the weeds, focused on leading a company day to day.

In the next four chapters, you are going to create a vision and plan for how you are going to invest your *time, talent, and treasure* going forward while simultaneously investing in your *Tribe*. This is about moving beyond who you are right here and right now, and actively owning the future that you have worked hard to create for yourself and those you love. This book includes the writing space to work through these areas.

As mentioned, you've probably heard of these buckets before, but as an entrepreneur, the way you need to process them as you exit your business and begin the next season of life is different.

Your Talent, Tribe, Time, and Treasure are the critical elements to developing your purpose beyond just being a business owner, and the way you define each of these things will evolve.

Your time has likely been greatly defined by your work schedule. Your talent has been defined by your contributions to your company. Your treasure has been defined by your salary, retirement nest-egg, and your company's bottom line. And your tribe has been defined often by work relationships getting much of your social capital.

This is all about to evolve. As a business owner with a desire to achieve a full, fun, and adventurous season of life after your exit, you have to think through each of these buckets with a very unique lens. This lens is that of a person who is incredibly driven, on the cusp of an amazing new season in life, has experienced great success, and still sees the opportunity for "more" in life.

> "You can't go back and change the beginning, but you can start where you are and change the ending."
>
> – C.S. Lewis

Word to the wise: To realize the best possible outcome using this process, you're going to need to create some peace and quiet in your head and heart. Each Reader will need to consider and find that place where you can do the best work. For some, that is a quiet room in a Library with your phone off. For others, it is a table in a coffee shop where there is comfortable background noise. We're all different, and sometimes it takes a few repetitions to get into an atmosphere where you can think clearly to start to gain some momentum. The bottom line is that you should not be caught off guard if the purpose of your next season of life doesn't just fall into your lap and onto the paper after ten minutes of thinking. Sometimes you need to plant some seeds and let them grow over time. Water these seeds with quiet time spent in thought and conversations with those you love, trust, and respect.

Timeline for completing the sojourner tools: Because the journey and the process is unique to each of us, there's no right or wrong answer to the questions the process poses. Working through this journey could take anywhere from two days to two months. Getting to the right answers depends a lot on how you are wired and think – and what you think the right answers are on the first pass may change as you revisit them over time. While there is no right or wrong, if you want the most meaningful benefit, *you will need to dig in and do the work*. This means being honest with yourself, and not shying away from hard topics or questions you may have.

> "When setting out on a journey do not seek advice from someone who never left home."
>
> – Rumi

Like many things you have experienced as a business owner, don't be surprised when your non-business owner friends or Family can't give you help on this. The good news is there are people who can, and we will discuss who they might be at the end of the book. Please be aware that as you ask yourself these hard questions, you are not alone – not the only one in the process of doing this. There are thousands of business owners who have walked this path and found purpose on the other side of their business leadership exit, and many who are doing it right now.

At the completion of the process, you will have defined where – in the next Season of your life – you will invest your unique *Talents*, with what *Tribe*, using how much of your available *Time* and what part of your *Treasure*.

Chapter 7

The TALENT Tool

It's well established that there are many types of assessment tools such as "StrengthsFinder™" that trained personnel provide to help individuals consider where their unique abilities lie. These types of assessments are numerous and outside the scope of this book. However, all these tools have one thing in common: they engage people in some way to take an inventory of yourself and how they relate to and ultimately impact the world around them.

However, as we covered in Chapter One, we also know that entrepreneurs like yourself are wired differently. Entrepreneurs preparing for the next season of life need to consider not only their unique abilities but also what to do with them and how best to harness the creative bandwidth and drive that energizes them. You may have some idea of what your unique abilities[3] are, but how do they translate into life after your exit from your business? That is the intent of the tools in the Sojourner Process™.

As I interviewed dozens of entrepreneurs while developing the Sojourner Process™, I asked them a simple question: "What is

---
[3] "Unique Ability 2.0 Discovery, Find your Best Self" by Dan Sullivan

your next season going to look like?" The answers mostly fell into one of a handful of buckets in which they want to organize their time:

ACTIVISM - Cause Based actions, leadership and investing. This would include founding 501-C3 entities.

COMPETITION – Activities for people who are 'wired to win' and are always looking for the next game in life.

FINANCIAL - Growing Your Personal Balance Sheet.

IMPACT - Community Based activities focused on 'giving back' in a variety of ways.

LEGACY - Family/Tribe Based activities, including growing your influence with others. This would include philanthropic endeavors.

PORTFOLIO - Your next Business Venture, whether early stage or mature, to whatever level you are involved.

THEOLOGICAL - Faith Based activities, such as mission trips, planting places of worship or leading classes.

OTHER – Yours may not fall easily into one of these.

(Exercise and Travel have been excluded from the categories in the matrix. I consider them "pay to play" – they are assumed to be included in what the next season includes. Unless you have serious goals in

these two areas that are beyond typical travel and physical exercise, I recommend leaving them out of this process.)

Let's dig a bit deeper.

ACTIVISM

Activism can simply be thought of as being a voice for furthering change or development in causes and topics you care about. This can include leadership, educating the public, Board service, investing, and more. Being an activist means taking your passion or care for something to the next level and committing to joining in on championing that cause or topic. It does not have to be political; you can use your voice to create change in countless arenas of life in both bold, public ways or quiet, private ways.

COMPETITION

Regardless of whether you play sports or enjoy winning a round of Euchre at family holidays, we are all wired to win in some way. Utilizing competition in the next season of your life often looks like taking your newfound time, energy, and resources and investing in areas of competition for the love of the challenge. This is an itch that, as a business owner, you may find you still need an outlet for years to come. Competition could mean participating in a "shark tank" competition at your local Chamber of Commerce, coaching youth sports, or getting involved with the College of Business at your local university and helping students develop business ideas.

FINANCIAL

When you exit your business, for many it becomes time to turn towards growing and maximizing their personal balance sheet. This is an opportunity to dream and develop goals for investments, real estate, and more than you may not have had the bandwidth to pursue while actively leading a Company. Diving into your finances with fresh eyes after your exit is also an inflection point that can create new connection points between family members or your spouse.

IMPACT

One of the most common responses to the sheer increase in the available time on the hands of former business owners is the desire to "make an impact". The good news is we all get to define "impact" in our own way.

One of those ways is via philanthropy. My daughter is a Philanthropic Advisor, and she sees firsthand the joy it brings individuals to give back to their community with their time and money. This joy seems to multiply when it is connected to the experiences your time as a business owner afforded you. Consider how your experiences have developed your passion for causes that are tied to your journey as a business owner within a given community. You may enjoy becoming one of the many Score advisors, who give back by allowing others to leverage their business wisdom (www.score.org).

LEGACY

The thing about Legacy is that if we aren't deliberate about defining what we want ours to be before we pass, we find that there won't be much of one at all. Those whose legacies make the biggest impact on the world when they are gone have spent time truly thinking about who they are and what they want the world to remember about their values. Your legacy can be developed through things like philanthropy and service, of course. However, the most powerful legacies often are built from a positive relational influence on others. The great Maya Angelou once said, "People will forget what you said, people will forget what you did, but people will never forget how you made them feel."

Considering and fully executing a plan around your legacy requires some deep thinking. If you wish to go another level deep on this topic, I highly recommend "The Ultimate Manual – The Missing Guide to Living the Meaningful Life" by Craig C. Sroda.

PORTFOLIO

If you are at the early stages of thinking about the next season of your life after your exit, it might seem premature to begin thinking about your next Business venture. However, mature these ventures might be, if they bring you energy and pique your interest you should not be afraid to follow your curiosity. It never hurts to take a phone call or set up a meeting about a business proposition.

THEOLOGICAL

Though not everyone reading this book will share the same faith, or faith at all, don't be surprised that your life after your exit may stir up deep questions in you. You might find yourself excited to dive back into your faith community, or you might find yourself prompted to think more about what you believe and what principles guide your inner life and core values. Regardless of where you fall on this spectrum, please embrace this aspect of your life. Inflection points in your life like this are an opportune time to reassess your values and life principles and how you live them out in a like-minded community. Don't miss the chance to invest in that.

INSTRUCTIONS FOR EXECUTING THE TALENT TOOL

After each of the four steps in the Sojourner Process™, you'll find some sample worksheets followed by a NOTES page for you to record your thoughts as you are brainstorming and casting your vision. In the appendices, you'll find clean ones to create your final version and you can also download full-page PDFs from www.exitwithandrew.com

1. Put today's date in the upper right corner. When you revisit this thinking, it will be good to have context tied to where you were.
2. To utilize the Talent Tool, the first step is to consider each of the above categories and to what extent your 'next season objectives' fall into that category.

Investing your TALENTs - WORKSHEET

TALENT CATEGORY	SPECIFIC OBJECTIVES	WHY?	Weight %
ACTIVISM - Cause Based action	All these years I have passed about local political leadership - am I ready to do something? Feels like a maybe	Luke 12:48b	10
COMPETITION - Your next game to Win	Complete 2 half marathons this year perhaps Indianapolis and Disney?	need to find a healthy way to scratch my competitive itch	5
FINANCIAL - Growing Your Balance Sheet	hmmm, I don't think much about this	I'm in a good place - trust Matt to watch & advise	0
IMPACT - Community Based/Giving Back	What about the school board? I have thought about that for a long time	great way to give back - leverage my help first mindset	40
LEGACY - Family/Tribe/Philanthropy Based	I will have the ability to go back to active status on the VOI Board	I can finish strong the commitment I started	10
PORTFOLIO - Your next Business Ventures	I'll have time to really dig in on that franchise model with Joe	I love the idea and his vision - how far am I willing to go...need to talk about this with KW	25
THEOLOGICAL - Faith Based activities	YES! Teach that Father Greg has been talking to me about! I don't know how much time this will take???		10
OTHER	Ok the more I think on this, the School Board just seems to jump out! But I have to get elected! How many times will I run? What can I do right now that doesn't require getting elected? I guess Coaching aligns with that? Who can I get to be my exploratory Committee? Dave & ROB? Who else?		
OTHER			
* Total Weighting should Equal 100%			100

NOTES

TALENT TOOL - PULLING IT ALL TOGETHER

Having dug deeper into each of these categories, some things should be jumping out at you – in fact, some may be screaming at you. Here are the next steps:

1. Take the top one or two outcomes you had from considering each section and fill them into the column labeled "Specific Objectives."
2. Having completed that, start back at the top and ask yourself "Why?" Ideally, the thinking process you have just been through will provide clarity on each one as to exactly why that reaches this level of importance for you. Fill that reason into the "Why?" column.
3. Finally, put a value, or 'weight' to each one – with the caveat that the total of the weighting must equal 100%. The principle here is that in this next Season, you have 100% of your *available* energy and bandwidth (which we'll determine later) to something – no more and no less. So go ahead and weigh each item.
4. Close the book and take a ten-minute break.

Conversely, there may be no alarms going off in your head, and no obvious answers coming into the light. That is completely fine – now is the point where you'll need to learn to get comfortable with being uncomfortable. There will be parts of this process that leave you a bit unsettled for a while. If this *doesn't happen* for you at some point along your sojourner journey, you may need to challenge yourself to go deeper.

If you are hitting a mental block, you may need to put the book away and give yourself a few days to process it mentally. Create an appointment on your calendar in 2 – 3 days to restart the process right here at Step One. In between now and then, if something comes to mind, pick up the book and re-engage here where you left off. If you come back and are still struggling, ask yourself why. What are the mental or emotional roadblocks stopping you from exploring these topics? (Recommended reference: https://www.clarityfieldguide.com/)

If you are interested in going deeper into this specific tool, I highly recommend the book "Strength to Strength" by Arthur C. Brooks. In his book, the author speaks to people he calls "Strivers", of which you as an entrepreneur are a unique subset.

Chapter 8

The TRIBE Tool

In this context, the word "Tribe" is used as a synonym for community. When you take a minute to consider, you will likely realize you have various sources and groups that represent "community" in your life. Prior to the pandemic, people were more community-oriented than they are now. The pandemic has served to force isolation, accelerate the work-from-home model, and the general acceptance of video meetings as a standard way of life. These things are not entirely bad, but they have brought about some unintended consequences after being incorporated into every element of our society.

If you are following (or are at least conscious of what is happening in) the world of artificial intelligence, it's safe to say that the emergence of AI and increased use of social media will irrevocably impact human culture going forward. This has shown us that genuine, in-person, face-to-face "community" is often harder and harder for people to find. Thomas Friedman talks about this in his book "Thank You for Being Late".

Based on where you are in your life and career trajectory, I'm hoping you're fortunate to have strong - and multiple - points of community available to you. The objective here is to think through what parts of your community you are going to choose to focus on in this next season.

I recently moved 90 minutes away to a new city. When this happened, I was caught off guard by how significantly the loss of certain elements of community impacted me. Whether you find community in your family, friends, gym, country club, faith community, or other, the most important fact to reckon with now is that after exiting your company, you can be sure it will no longer be found at that location. That's harder for some to deal with than others, but it brings challenges for everyone - no matter who you are.

Ideally, the process of thinking through your talents in the prior section, along with where and how you would like to exercise those, may have shed some early light on this Tribe question. Use those realizations as filters to help you identify - by name - which parts of your life are a community that you would like to impact.

INSTRUCTIONS FOR EXECUTING THE TRIBE TOOL

1) Put today's date in the upper right corner. When you revisit this thinking, it will be good to have context tied to where you were.

2) Begin by listing a brainstorm of all the areas of community currently in your life.

3) Then, in the next column, ask yourself "Why do I think of this group as part of my Tribe?"

4) Then ask yourself "What is my ideal relationship with this Tribe?" For example, I have a goal of getting to my gym three times per week at a certain time because I know there's a group of young entrepreneurs that work out then and I'm able to have fun discussions that I believe are having a positive impact on them as well.

5) Then, based on that ideal relationship, ask yourself "What are the actions I need to take to achieve that?"

Before you begin, here is some encouragement: if you look at the tool below and struggle to think of a variety of communities you'd like to impact, know that you are not alone. As I mentioned earlier, it is critical to acknowledge the impact the pandemic has had on our sense of community. For some, it completely eliminated any sense of community they had. If you find yourself struggling to create a list, turn the question around: to thrive in your life after you exit your company, what areas of community would you like to _add_ to your life? Think about who your ideal Tribe would be and why. Maybe it's a new group of friends or fellow entrepreneurs, or maybe it's a new faith community or athletic club. In any case, spend some time thinking about what areas of your Tribe are missing and what might fill those gaps.

TRIBE

Name	WHY Are They Tribe?	IDEAL RELATIONSHIP	ACTIONS TO TAKE
My Crew	They're my blessings & gifts	make a great thing better by being emotionally present	Get clarity on what it means to be true Father and live it!
The School	I wouldn't be who I am without them	Board member and/or Coach	Frame up a run for the Board either way I can coach
Extended Family	Honoring Grandma & Grandpa	Manage the Family reunion	Sort out the planning committee what if only I feel this way?
SJOC Parish	They've given me a future	Full freedom to lead and serve as called on	Increase $$ giving; Increase teaching time
Crossfit Gym	Kept me going thru covid	athete & mentor	3-4x per week; coffee meets outside of class

NOTES

Chapter 9

The TIME Tool

There are hundreds of books in existence about time management. In your career, you've also likely been to at least two seminars on this subject. You know the clichés about time management and also know that many of them are true.

Readers of this book are part of a very small percentage of people who have businesses they are planning to exit and therefore will likely have the flexibility of time that most people can only dream of. You have the luxury of using it, however you would like. We are going to use the term "significant time" to highlight the reality that you have the freedom to use this time in the way that you determine will have the biggest and boldest impact on your Tribe. The alternative option is to fritter it away.

The intention is not to give you a new or additional time management tool. Rather, it is to help you realize and prioritize the use of your "significant time" for this next season of your life.

As you consider this, having completed both the Talent and Tribe filters, I hope that you are coming to conclusions on each topic that align with one another. These different filters often show us the same two or three themes from multiple angles - the commonalities between each tool are what you should pay attention to. For example, you find that a Talent that you are highly gifted at will significantly impact a certain segment of your tribe or community. You may also find a Talent you have, which you are still growing and building is truly needed by a group within your Tribe right now. These throughlines will not only bring you the largest sense of growth and satisfaction...they will impact those around you the most as well.

The most important thing to do with your time after you exit your business is to be intentional with it...more intentional than you have ever been. Without intention, time will float by and you will miss the opportunity to use this <u>season of maximum impact</u> on your Tribes.

To use this tool, list the Tribes you would like to impact in column one. In column two, list which of your Talents are best leveraged by investing Time here. In column three, ask yourself (realistically!) how many hours per month you are willing to invest or pour into each of the Tribes you have listed.

INSTRUCTIONS FOR EXECUTING THE TIME TOOL

1) Put today's date in the upper right corner. When you revisit this thinking, it will be good to have context tied to where you were.

2) Begin by listing the Tribes you would like to make an impact on.

3) Then, in the next column, flip back to the Talent tool and list which of your Talents are best leveraged by investing Time here.

4) In column three, ask yourself – realistically – how many hours per month you are prepared to invest.

5) At the bottom, sum up the number of hours per month you believe you would like to invest in each. This will enable you to create a schedule that holds you accountable to your desires to invest your precious time to grow personally and make an impact on these Tribes.

TIME - Your LIFE

TRIBES TO IMPACT	WHICH TALENTS IMPACT	HRS per MONTH	IDEAS and THOUGHTS
School	Coaching & Board Leadership	60	What is my role if I'm not elected?
Rotary Club	Giving back: Leadership	10	75% of meetings and volunteer projects
Board meetings	Leadership & vision	10	To back to VOI? Which others?
Parish Life	Coaching, teaching	25	Class teaching, prep & outside meetings
Humane Society volunteer	A giving heart & vision	5	Away to say thanks for Piper
Start up Business with Joe	I love this cause!	20	
	Ok, but what is my amount I'm willing to commit? 30 hrs/wk?		
TOTAL		130	

NOTES

Chapter 10

The TREASURE Tool

As you have gone about your Entrepreneurial journey, it's likely you've partnered with a great financial planner and have a good plan or roadmap in place for your personal wealth. Truth be told, not all my clients have one when we begin preparing for an exit. If you are one of those who have not, it's time to initiate that process in parallel to the Sojourner Process ™. If you need help with that, you'll find comments on the resources pages.

The context for the Treasure tool is that, given the discoveries you have made in your Talent, Tribe, and Time tools, you should have some clarity on where you may want to invest your charitable giving, or your 'Treasure', so that it has the greatest impact on your defined Tribes.

My daughter works as a Philanthropic Advisor for a major bank, helping high-net and ultra-high-net-worth families and individuals give away their charitable funds with intention and impact. We talk about the idea of investing your treasure and aligning it with your values frequently. She sees people who do so just to get the tax break, and she sees people give their treasure and find immense joy in the process. There are many families and individuals that have experienced a wealth event, often from the sale of a business, and have no idea how to start when it comes to giving money away strategically. Most of my daughters' clients find that this gets easier and much more fun when they are able to identify alignment between their core values and organizations that share these core values. These could be groups connected to your Tribe or groups that you find through some simple online research. By aligning discretionary philanthropic giving to them, you will find greater connectivity to your Tribe and your own values.

This idea assumes that you have identified and are leveraging your core values. From my client experience, Entrepreneurs and their companies fall into one of three groups:

1. They have not done any core value discovery work;
2. They have the core values on a sign in the lobby, but they have little if any impact on day-to-day business operations;
3. or they have identified their core values and are actively leveraging them to hire, fire, recognize, and reward based on those values.

Depending upon which of these groups you feel you are in, your route to leveraging this tool will be different. If you are in the camp of never having done a core values discovery exercise you may find that extremely helpful. There are numerous resources available online, here is one example: www.discoveryourvalues.com/tvd. This step cannot be skipped, and I would encourage you to involve your family, loved ones, and your business leadership in the process.

If you either have not done core values discovery work or are in the camp where it is simply given lip service but not truly lived out, I want to encourage you to dig in and do the work in the near future. What would it look like to make changes in your life, business, relationships, and giving to reflect those values? I think you will find that the joy and perspective aligning your giving with your values is priceless.

Lastly, if you are actively using core values in your business today and they are a foundational element of who you and your company are, then let's go forward. In the left-hand column of the table below, write your core values. In the next column, include which groups or people in your Tribes align with those core values. In the third column, identify what amount of 'Treasure' you may be willing to provide to those groups.

<u>Ultimately, the objective here is to take a holistic approach to aligning use of your Treasure to where you intend to have the most significant impact on your Tribes, leveraging your unique Talents and available Time commitment.</u>

INSTRUCTIONS FOR EXECUTING THE TREASURE TOOL

1) Put today's date in the upper right corner. When you revisit this thinking, it will be good to have context tied to where you were.

2) Begin by listing your Tribes that you identified in the earlier work.

3) Then, in the next column, list the Core values that come to mind when you think about why those tribes are part of your life

4) In column three, ask yourself what type of financial commitment you are willing and able to make.

5) At the bottom, sum the value of these proposed contributions. Do these align with your overall financial plan? If not, don't make the commitment.

6) Finally, make any notes or comments to yourself as a reminder of why you landed on these Tribes and financial numbers.

TREASURE

KEY TRIBE	CORE VALUE ALIGNMENT	DOLLARS/MO.	IDEAS / THOUGHTS
School	Pay it forward	$500	Is the excellence committee the only way to give?
Rotary	Impacting the world for good	$250	Honoring Grandpa makes me happy!
Parish	Love God, love others	$2000	I have been blessed & now have the ability to give back
Humane Society	Loving God's creation	$200	not just giving my time
Strangers	Love God, Love others	$250	Plan out random acts of kindness
TOTAL		$3200	

NOTES

Chapter 11

Stepping into the Next Season

No matter what your experience with the Sojourner Process ™ has felt like to this moment, please note that the important thing is that this 'in-between' moment won't last forever. Before we began this process, remember that we defined being a Sojourner as the following:

"Once you have first begun thinking about exiting your current company, you are officially a "Sojourner." A Sojourner is defined as someone who is "staying as a temporary resident." Though you are beginning this journey into a place of unknown and personal reflection now, the objective is to not stay where you are – this is a temporary stop on your way to living out the vision you will take some time to create."

After spending time with each of the four tools, it is up to you to assess if you need more time working through these concepts, or if you are ready to take steps to prepare for the exit from your company. The important thing to remember is that in either case, you have already done what *most* business owners do not do: take

<u>the first step</u> in moving with intention towards the next season of your life.

Remind yourself what kind of life we're talking about here: one in which you exit your company and then accelerate into the next season <u>*because you know what your purpose is beyond your company*</u>. Living with this life in mind will continue to motivate you as you phase out of the Sojourner Process™.

No matter what level of clarity you have at this moment, please embrace that you are not the same person you were when you began this process. That internal change, and the creation of a vision for the next season of your life, will pay you dividends beyond what you can imagine.

Though the next step may still feel unclear or unknown, you can continually return to the tools within the Sojourner Process™ to light the way and discern the next steps in your journey. Maybe that next step is engaging an Exit Planner or an M&A Advisor. Maybe that next step includes setting a date – perhaps one year from now - where you will re-evaluate your readiness to sell your company. Maybe the next step is to read one of the many books and resources mentioned in this book.

Regardless of what it looks like, I hope you allow yourself to feel proud, and full of anticipation, as you look at the hard internal work you have done and continue to dream about what lies ahead of you.

The end of the Sojourner Process™ isn't another step or tool (though we will conclude in the next chapter with some practical next steps). It is the freedom to use the beginnings of the vision you created during the process to continue to propel yourself forward into the Next Season of your Life. Embrace the next stage of sojourning into that season with newfound purpose.

I know it will be full, fun, purpose-driven, fulfilling, and joyful.

CONCLUSION

If you were willing to dig in and do the challenging work of the Sojourner Process™, it is highly unlikely you will be part of the 75% of entrepreneurs who reported being unhappy with their exit plan. Your willingness to engage and do this hard work makes you unique among Entrepreneurs.

As we conclude, let's circle back to where we started: ***You are bigger and much more important to the world than the company you run.***

I want to leave you with some ideas for the next steps to launch you into your future.

1. Once the Sojourner tools are completed, review the work you completed in your "Shareholder vs Stakeholder" exercise and have a conversation with the appropriate individuals. How and why do these people fit into the categories you thought through?

2. If there are actions required to fully resolve your Shareholder/Stakeholder list, reach out to an exit planner.

3. Have a conversation with your Spouse, partner, or appropriate family members about what you have learned about yourself in your Sojourner Process™ and share your vision for the next Season of your life. This can often be concurrent with item two above, but not always.

4. Arrange at least three coffee or lunch meetings with people from your different "Tribes". Explain the work you have done here and discuss your vision for how you would like to engage with the Tribe.

5. Start small and choose ONE item from your Time list and begin consistently engaging that way over the next 60 days to determine if you are on the right track, or perhaps need to rethink this use of your Time.

6. Finally, please *reach out to me* at andrew@exitwithandrew.com. I would love to hear how the process and tools worked for you.

As you might imagine, there are thousands of Entrepreneurs like you who are at a similar place in their lives. While our world is more and more "connected", fewer and fewer people are truly "connecting". Post-pandemic, social media often feeds into the isolation many people experience. As a result, my hope is that this book will create a place of Community and connection for other Entrepreneurs going through the same process that you are.

If you would like to engage with a community of people like yourself who are journeying through the concepts in this book, head to www.lifeonthetable.net and leave a Testimonial for how the Sojourner Process™ has impacted you. There you will find names and comments from others who may be experiencing the same questions, struggles, and joys as you throughout this process.

As you finish this book, you may *not have* reached a point of clarity. If you have reached this chapter lacking certainty and feel like you need additional help, I'm happy to talk and help work through whatever roadblock you may have encountered. Additionally, I have connected with many great Business Coaches who can help you further in your journey, and I would love to connect you with them. Please use my email address above.

If this journey has convinced you that it is time for you to move into actively selling your company, please check out the Epilogue, where I share what I believe are some critical things you should know. Many entrepreneurs only do this once, so let's make sure that it's a positive experience for you.

Finally – thank you for embarking on this literal "road less traveled" by entrepreneurs. I truly believe that to the extent Entrepreneurs will embrace leaving their companies to embrace the 'next great thing', the world will be a better place due to what you are about to achieve next!

EPILOGUE

If You're Getting Ready To Sell

I imagine that a large percentage of the readers of this book are golfers. When you want to improve your golf game and are serious, you hire a teaching pro and invest time in taking lessons. Why? Because golf is a hard game, particularly hard to get better at just by reading books or golf digest and hammering balls at a driving range. I'm here to tell you that hiring a Coach(es) for your transition is not only no different *but also more important.*

Consider things in life that are critical to your growth, and I'm willing to bet you've hired a coach to help you through them. Business peer groups such as YPO, Renaissance Executive Forums. Vistage, EO, C12, and others fall under this heading. In fact, if you're anything like me you've probably also hired a coach to give you some therapy and help you through some of life's more challenging experiences.

When it comes time to sell one of the most valuable assets you may ever own, I recommend that you hire an expert to help you do it. The nature of these transactions is complicated, emotional, and nuanced, and it is amazing to me when people decide that this is a good thing to try to do on their own. <u>Please engage both an Exit Planner and M&A advisor.</u>

I can tell you with certainty from my experience that a good transaction Advisor will easily cover their fee on one or more of the negotiations. That ignores all the other points of value that they will provide along the way. Most importantly, the ROI or value of the market competition we create is literally priceless. Ask yourself – if the advisor's fee is (hypothetically) 4% of the consideration paid, don't you believe that an experienced professional can deliver a 4% better outcome than you can?

If you want your exit process to have the best possible outcome with minimum stress, hire a transaction coach - hire an investment banker or M & A advisor. Their job is to help you not "leave money on the table", as the saying goes.

If you have questions, please email me as outlined in Chapter 12.

ACKNOWLEDGEMENTS

This book is the outcome of a lifetime of relationships. So, finding a way to acknowledge everyone who contributed in any way was challenging. It's my pleasure to thank these 'tribes' that have been part of my story:

This would not have happened without my amazing wife, Kristin, whose love gave me both the wings and the roots that I needed to execute this project. It's not possible to thank you enough!

To Mom and Dad – I can't thank you enough for everything… I won the lottery the day I was born to you.

To my original tribe: Nicholas, Madeleine, and Isabelle…and now also Madison, Fran, and Carter. I love you all – you make my heart sing. A special thank you to Maddie for being my editor and pushing me through this project.

To Matt, Ellen, and my Williams and Whiteman family tribe… I love you and am so thankful for all of you.

To my tribe of descendants of Harold and Dorothy Wible – I am the person I am today because of you all. Thanks to you.

There's a sign in my parents' house that says "It takes a long time to grow old friends". I have a great tribe of friends - thank you to all of you. Thanks to Chris and Tina for saving my life. Thanks to Dave and Rob for always walking alongside me to make sure I put that life to good use.

To Anna, Caroline, and Lauren – thanks for giving me a chance.

And finally, to Father Gregory and my tribe at Saint Joseph Orthodox Church, thank you for always being there.

RESOURCES

Books Referenced in the text:

"Man's Search for Meaning", Frankl, Viktor
ISBN: 978-0807014271

"Driven: Understanding and Harnessing the Genetic Gifts Shared by Entrepreneurs, Navy SEALs, Pro Athletes, and Maybe You" Brackmann, Douglass
ISBN: 978-1619616936

"Quit - The Power of Knowing When to Walk Away", Duke, Annie
ISBN: 978-0593422991

"Willing Wisdom", Deans, Thomas William
ISBN: 978-0980891027

"Unique Ability 2.0 Discovery, Find your Best Self" Sullivan, Dan
ISBN: 978-1897239414

"The Ultimate Manual – the missing guide to living the meaningful life" Sroda, Craig
ISBN 978-1-73287080-0-2

"Strength to Strength" Brooks, Arthur
ISBN 978-0-593-19148-4

Andrew's website: www.exitwithandrew.com
https://www.linkedin.com/in/exit-with-andrew/

APPENDIX A
<u>SHAREHOLDERS TOOL</u>

APPENDIX B
STAKEHOLDERS TOOL

APPENDIX C
TALENT TOOL

Investing your TALENTs - WORKSHEET

TALENT CATEGORY	SPECIFIC OBJECTIVES	WHY?	Weight %
ACTIVISM - Cause Based action			
COMPETITION - Your next game to Win			
FINANCIAL - Growing Your Balance Sheet			
IMPACT - Community Based/Giving Back			
LEGACY - Family/Tribe/Philanthropy Based			
PORTFOLIO - Your next Business Ventures			
THEOLOGICAL - Faith Based activities			
OTHER			
OTHER			
OTHER			

* Total Weighting should Equal 100%

APPENDIX D
TRIBE TOOL

APPENDIX E
TIME TOOL

TOTAL										TRIBES TO IMPACT	TIME - Your LIFE
										WHICH TALENTS IMPACT	
										HRS per MONTH	
										IDEAS and THOUGHTS	

APPENDIX F
TREASURE TOOL

TOTAL										KEY TRIBE	TREASURE
										CORE VALUE ALIGNMENT	
										DOLLARS/MO.	
										IDEAS / THOUGHTS	